Steck-Vaughn

Think-Alongs™

Comprehending As You Read

Level D

Program Authors

Senior Author
Roger Farr

Co-Authors
Jennifer Conner
Elizabeth Haydel
Bruce Tone
Beth Greene
Tanja Bisesi
Cheryl Gilliland

STECK-VAUGHN®
COMPANY

A Division of Harcourt Brace & Company

www.steck-vaughn.com

Acknowledgments

Editorial Director	Diane Schnell
Project Editor	Anne Souby
Associate Director of Design	Cynthia Ellis
Design Manager	Ted Krause
Production and Design	Julia Miracle-Hagaman
Photo Editor	Claudette Landry
Product Manager	Patricia Colacino
Cover Design	Ted Krause
Cover Sculpture	Lonnie Springer
Cover Production	Alan Klemp

Think-Alongs™ is a trademark of Steck-Vaughn Company.

ISBN 0-7398-0086-8

1 2 3 4 5 6 7 8 9 0   PO   03 02 01 00 99

Contents

Thinking About

Causes and Effects

Read the selection below. As you read, think about what causes other things to happen. Also think about the effects of certain events and actions.

Jeff was nervous as he approached the plate for his turn at bat. He could hear his family and friends cheering him on. Hearing them made him want to hit that ball farther than he ever had.

This was the championship game. His team was down one run in the bottom of the ninth inning. There were two outs and the bases were loaded. His team was counting on him.

Jeff waited for the ball. Whack! It flew high and far! He had hit a home run!

As Jeff ran the bases, the crowd chanted his name, "Jeff! Jeff! Jeff!" Jeff swelled with pride. His team had won the game!

Did you think about causes and effects as you read?

I was glad Jeff hit a home run. He helped his team win the game.

Answer the questions below.

- What caused Jeff to be nervous?

_____

- What effect did the crowd have on Jeff?

_____

- What caused the crowd to chant Jeff's name?

_____

_____

What other causes and effects did you think of as you read?

_____

_____

_____

_____

Read and Think

- Read the selections that follow.
- Stop at each box and answer the question.
- Remember to think about causes and effects.

To the Rescue!

By Linda Rae Apolzon

This selection is about three boys who try to save a duck in trouble. Read the selection to find out what the duck needs and whether the boys are able to save it.

When we got to the pond that Friday afternoon, summer sunshine was making the water sparkle. A blue jay screeched at us. Tyler—he's my little brother—croaked at a frog.

Tyler is only five, but he goes everywhere with me and my friend John. My mom started a business at home last summer. Now every day she says to me, "Mike, if you and John could just watch Tyler, that would be . . . "

". . . a big help," I always answer. "I know. Come on, Tyler."

1 How do you think Mike feels about Tyler going with him everywhere?

It's a nice little pond, not deep or anything, so I'm allowed to go there without a grownup. That day, though, it wasn't so nice. Someone had left cans all over.

"Slobs," John mumbled, picking up cans.

I rinsed them in the water before putting them in my backpack, because I didn't want it to be sticky. I was mad. I mean, it's not our pond—it belongs to the college where Dad teaches. But still.

2 When people throw cans around the pond, how are other people affected?

I finished rinsing and stood up. Then I froze. "John," I said, "look at that duck."

Near the edge of the pond, a duck was swimming in circles. I could tell by his long, pointy tail feathers and long neck that he was a male pintail. He dipped his bill into the water, then tipped his head back and gulped. One ring of a plastic six-pack holder was around his neck. I wondered how the bird could swallow. Another ring was around one of his wings, keeping him from flying.

3   How might the duck have been caught in the plastic six-pack holder?

He was pretty close to me, so I dived for him. Unfortunately I don't get much practice tackling ducks. The pintail paddled away in panic. Tyler watched and worried. "Mike, we're not allowed to swim in the pond," he said.

"Mike wasn't swimming," said John. "He was trying to catch that duck so we can get those plastic rings off. If we don't, the duck might starve or get caught by a predator."

John thought he could chase the pintail toward me if I stood as still as I could. John circled the pond, trying to direct the duck. Tyler wiggled around. He kept giving us advice. "Ducks are fast, so you have to move *quick*."

"Quick, Tyler. Right. Now, shhhh."

The duck drifted nearer to me. John splashed toward him from the opposite side of the pond. Tyler jumped up and down on the muddy shore. I grabbed for the duck when he was close enough. The pintail slipped away by jumping into the air, but then he plopped right back down again. Quickly, he swam away. By this time, Tyler had fallen in the mud.

4 What do you think will happen to the duck if no one can help it?

It went on like that all afternoon. Finally we gave up and trudged home. All three of us were wet and muddy and smelled like pond scum. Our parents weren't going to be happy.

I told Dad about the duck. He frowned. Then he said, "We need something to catch him with. How about an old sheet?"

The next morning we—including Dad, who was all excited about the plan—headed for the pond. We took a sheet, scissors (for cutting the six-pack holder), and a bag of corn. When we threw some corn into the pond, ducks and geese charged at it.

"Now throw some on the shore," Dad said. A couple of mallards waddled up to eat the corn. So did our pintail.

5   Why do you think the boys are trying so hard to help the duck?

John got more corn ready while Dad and I unfolded the sheet. Tyler kept whispering "Shhhh!" The pintail was right in front of us, next to the mallards. Dad and I raised the sheet.

"Quick!"

"Quack!"

We got him! Under the sheet, the duck flapped furiously. "Dad?" said Tyler.

"Not now," Dad replied. We unwrapped our catch and found—a female mallard. Tyler pointed to the pond. Bobbing on the water was our pintail. He eyed us suspiciously and kept his distance from us.

"Stinky luck," said Tyler.

We spent the rest of the day there. All I can say is that the geese and ducks had a feast—except for our pintail. He was spooked and wouldn't come close. By the time we left, he was at the other end of the pond, not moving much. How long had he been tangled in those rings? How long would he be able to survive?

 6 How do you think the boys felt when they didn't catch the pintail?

Next day there were thunderstorms, and Mom kept us home. On Monday Dad said he'd go with us after lunch. We got more corn ready.

I didn't know what we'd find—if anything. Had the duck been caught and eaten? Even Tyler was quiet as he, John, and I got near the pond. Then I stopped in my tracks.

There was our pintail with his back to us. He was nibbling at something on land. Dad had the sheet, but he was too far behind us to help. I looked at John, and he nodded. The two of us got between the duck and the water. I signaled, and we both rushed toward him.

All I saw were gray webbed feet and grabbing hands. Then we heard Tyler screaming from the edge of the pond, "I got him! I got him!"

Good old Tyler. Dad raced over and held the duck with the sheet while John got the scissors. The most fun I ever had was cutting off that plastic holder.

The duck didn't even try to get loose—he was probably weak from hunger. We walked him to the water, set him down, and he slipped in. He swam around for a few minutes, just relaxing. Then he started dipping into the water and pulling up plants and stuff to eat.

I cut that six-pack holder into a zillion pieces and put every one of them in my backpack. Then John, Tyler, and I sat down on the grass. Dad grinned at us.

Bright sunshine made the water sparkle. Tyler croaked at a frog. Everything was back the way it should be. I felt good.

7 How do you think Tyler's big brother feels about him now?

Littering is a problem almost everywhere.

- For this activity, you will write a letter to the editor of your local newspaper. Explain why people should not litter. Also, tell how you think your city or neighborhood can get people to stop littering.

Prewriting

First, think about what you are going to write.

Reasons why littering is a problem:

_____

_____

_____

_____

Suggestions of how to get people to stop littering:

_____

_____

_____

_____

_____

Writing

Now, use another sheet of paper to write your letter.

Begin your letter with "Dear Editor."

Helen Keller

By David A. Adler

This selection tells about the life of a famous woman named Helen Keller. Read the selection to find out what Helen Keller did that made her so famous.

Helen Keller was born in Tuscumbia, Alabama on June 27, 1880. She was a pretty baby. She was happy and smart.

When Helen was just six months old, she began talking. But a year later, in February 1882, she became sick. She had a high fever. Her parents and doctors were afraid she would die.

Helen's mother held her and placed wet towels on Helen's forehead to cool the fever. After a few days the illness was gone.

But Helen had changed. She turned away from bright lights. She didn't hear people when they spoke to her. The illness had left Helen Keller blind and deaf. The world for her became forever dark and quiet.

 1 What are you thinking about now?

Because Helen could not hear other people speak, she did not learn to talk herself. She forgot the few words she knew as a baby. Helen did things with her hands to tell people what she wanted. Helen pretended to tie her hair in a bun if she wanted her mother. She pretended to cut and butter a slice of bread if she wanted bread.

Helen held onto her mother's dress as her mother walked through the house. Helen touched things to know how they felt and how they were shaped.

There must have been many things Helen wanted to do, many things she wanted to say, but she couldn't. Helen was often angry. She kicked, screamed, and cried.

2 Why do you think Helen Keller was so angry?

Helen was also mischievous. Once she locked her mother in the pantry. Another time she cut off all her friend's hair.

Helen's parents took her to eye doctors. But nothing could be done to help Helen see again.

Then Helen's parents took her to Washington, D.C. to meet Alexander Graham Bell, the inventor of the telephone. Dr. Bell had once taught in a school for the deaf. He helped the Kellers find a teacher for Helen.

The teacher they found was Anne Mansfield Sullivan. Helen first met her on March 3, 1887. Helen called that day her "soul's birthday."

3 Why do you think she called that day her "soul's birthday"?

Helen was not an easy student. Once, in a fit of anger, she knocked out two of Anne Sullivan's teeth.

First Anne Sullivan taught Helen proper manners. Then she taught her words.

Anne used a finger alphabet. She gave Helen a doll and spelled "d-o-l-l" in the palm of Helen's hand. She gave Helen a hat and spelled "h-a-t" in her hand. But Helen did not understand.

One day Anne and Helen passed a water pump. Anne took Helen's hand and put it under the water. In Helen's other hand Anne spelled "w-a-t-e-r."

Now Helen understood. Everything has a name.

 4   What are you thinking about now?

Helen wanted to learn more. That day she learned the words "mother" and "father." She also learned "teacher" which is what she called Anne Sullivan.

Many years later Helen Keller wrote that learning "water," her first word, gave her soul light, hope, and joy.

Helen learned hundreds, then thousands of words.

Soon Anne Sullivan taught Helen to read by feeling patterns of raised dots on paper. This kind of writing for the blind is called Braille.

Helen learned so much and so fast that she became famous throughout the world. She was called "the wonder girl."

 5 Why do you think people called Helen Keller "the wonder girl"?

When Helen was ten she decided she would learn to speak. But Helen couldn't hear the sounds she was making. She did learn to speak, but not clearly.

In 1900 Helen became a college student. She went to Radcliffe College. Anne Sullivan sat next to her and spelled in Helen's hand everything that was said in class. Helen was an excellent student. While she was in college, she wrote *The Story of My Life*, which was read by people throughout the world. Helen graduated with honors in 1904.

Helen wrote more articles and books about her life, her teacher, and how she learned. She and Anne Sullivan lectured before large audiences.

6 What are you thinking about now?

Anne Sullivan died on October 20, 1936. She had been with Helen for almost fifty years. After Anne's death, Polly Thomson, Helen's secretary since 1914, became her constant companion.

Helen worked all her life to help others, especially blind people. She worked for many years for the American Foundation for the Blind.

During the Second World War, Helen Keller visited injured soldiers in hospitals. Her visits meant a lot to the soldiers. Many of them had been blinded or had lost their hearing in the fighting. Helen Keller brought them hope. They would try to lead useful lives despite their disabilities, just like Helen Keller.

Important people wanted to meet Helen Keller. She met kings, queens, and presidents. She met actors, writers, and scientists.

 7   Why did so many people want to meet Helen Keller?

People, universities, and governments all over the world gave Helen Keller awards. In 1964 President Lyndon Johnson gave her the Presidential Medal of Freedom.

Helen Keller died on June 1, 1968.

Helen Keller couldn't see or hear, but for more than eighty years she had always been busy. She read and wrote books. She learned how to swim and even how to ride a bicycle. She did many things well. But most of all, Helen Keller brought hope and love to millions of people with disabilities.

8   How do you think she brought hope to people with disabilities?

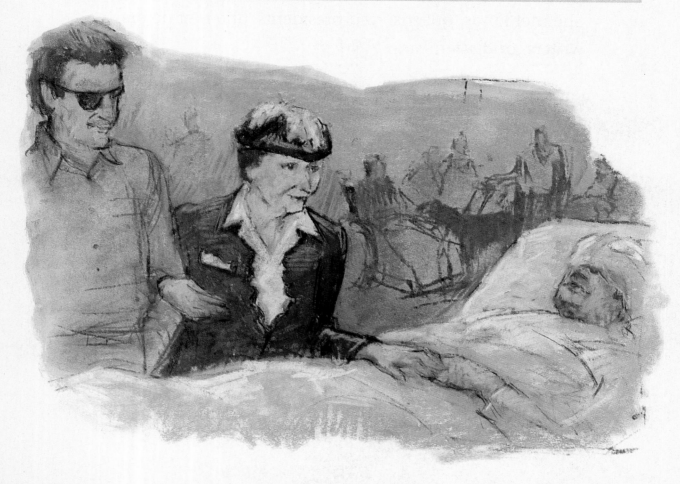

Time to Write!

Helen Keller inspired many people. She showed them what they could do. Think of someone who inspires you.

• For this activity, you will write a letter to that person telling why you are inspired by him or her.

Prewriting

First, think about what you want to include in your letter.

What does it mean for a person to inspire others?

_____

_____

_____

Who inspires you? _____

Why does the person inspire you?

_____

_____

_____

_____

Writing

Now, use another sheet of paper to write your letter.

25

THE TINY KITE OF EDDIE WING

By Maxine Trottier

This selection is about a boy who dreams of flying a kite, and the old man who helps him reach his dream. Read the selection to find out how and why the old man helps Eddie Wing.

Once there was a small boy named Eddie Wing.
He lived in a city of tall hills by a bay. His home was
above a flower stall and each day he helped his parents
at their work. His mother and father loved him very
much, but they worried over him. From the moment
Eddie got up until the moment he went to sleep, he
thought of nothing but kites.

Like most of the people on their street, the Wing family was very poor. Though Eddie could dream of fine silk kites, there was no money for even the smallest paper kite. So, Eddie made do with his dreams.

 1 Why did Eddie spend so much time dreaming?

Every day after the flower stall was closed, Eddie Wing would climb to the top of the city's highest hills. There, he would run through the grass holding an imaginary string in one hand. With the other hand he would pull on the invisible cord and urge a kite that only he could see up into the cold, blue sky. At first the other children laughed. Then they stopped to watch. Finally one day, they all ran behind Eddie, cheering for the kite that they could *almost* see.

 2 Why can't anyone see this kite?

Eddie's favorite event of the year was The Festival of Kites. He had watched the competitions ever since he could remember. And ever since he could remember, a prize had been offered by Old Chan. Chan was the most prosperous man in the whole neighborhood. He owned a large restaurant and a store. Everyone who passed him in the street stopped and bowed.

Of course, Old Chan no longer worked in his restaurant. He only sat outside the store and thought about the days before he was so important—when he was a little boy in China with his whole life ahead of him.

In those days he had his own dream. He had wanted to be a poet. But when his family sailed across the sea to make a new start, there was not time for poetry. Chan's dream lay hidden like a tiny seed that has been planted, but never watered.

 3 What are you thinking about now?

It was Chan who made up the test for The Festival of Kites each summer. One year it was for the fastest kite. Another time it was for the kite with the longest tail. No one knew from year to year what challenge Old Chan would set before them, but as the days grew longer and warmer, he could be seen sitting in the sun outside his store, thinking.

"He is deciding about The Festival of Kites," everyone would say, and sometimes he was. But more often than not, he made up small, secret poems inside his head, poems he never wrote down.

4   What do you think the test this year will be?

Eddie Wing could barely sleep the night before Old Chan announced this year's challenge. When he closed his eyes he saw colored shapes drifting in his small room above the flower stall. All night long the snap of kite tails filled his ears.

Finally morning came, and as he always did, Old Chan announced his challenge.

"This year," he said, "the prize will not be for the fastest kite. It will not be for the biggest kite, or the one with the longest tail. This year the prize can only go to the kite that is smaller than any other." Then Chan sat back down to enjoy the sun and to doze. Before he slept, he made up a secret poem about tiny flying things. Unwritten, it drifted about in his sleepy head before floating away forever.

At once, people began working on their kites. They bought thin cord and short, light sticks. Those who could not afford silk bought colored paper.

But Eddie did not even have the money for that. Each day he helped his parents with the flowers, and each afternoon he climbed the tallest hill in the city. There, with all the other children running behind him, he flew his dream kite.

On the day of The Festival of Kites, the sun shone and a fine, strong wind blew just as it should. With Old Chan leading the way, everyone climbed to the top of the highest hill. One by one, the people launched their kites until the sky was filled with swooping color.

 5   What are you thinking about now?

Each kite was smaller than the last. Tiny jewels of silk and paper shivered and danced in the sunlight. It seemed impossible that such delicate things could hold together in the wind, but Old Chan knew they would.

Then Chan noticed Eddie. "That boy," he said. "What is that boy doing? He is flying an invisible kite." For off a little way from everyone else ran Eddie Wing with the other children behind him.

At first all the people laughed as the boy urged his dream kite higher into the sky. Then they stopped and watched. Later on, some of them admitted to their friends that they *might* have seen something tiny and bright and clear riding high in the sky over the bay.

Old Chan knew better. He gave the prize to a girl who had flown a very small kite indeed. It was amazing that such a tiny seed of a thing could catch enough wind to fly.

 6   Why did the girl win the prize?

But, as everyone walked back down the hill to eat and drink at the festival, Old Chan beckoned to Eddie. "Come with me," he said.

Together, they walked through the streets to the door of Chan's store. They went inside, and after much digging and moving and crinkling of paper, the old man handed Eddie Wing a parcel.

"Yours was a very tiny kite; too small to actually see. You know, you must try to do something about that."

Eddie began to open the parcel, but Old Chan stopped him. "Run along, boy: I feel a poem coming on."

When Eddie got home, he opened the parcel by himself. In the stiff, red paper lay a length of silk, some light sticks, and a ball of cord.

A few days later across the highest hill, all the children were running behind Eddie Wing once more. Now though, his kite could be seen by everyone, and it was a beautiful kite indeed.

爺娘無錢買紫朱
何來錢幣備紙線
舉頭家望鄰紙鳶
空空兩手有誰憐

As for Old Chan, well, he went back to his chair in the sun. In his head he made up a poem about the little boy who flew a tiny kite of dreams, a kite of air as small as a seed. But this time, before the poem could float away, Chan took up a brush and wrote it down.

7 What are you thinking about now?

Time to Write!

Eddie dreamed of flying kites. Old Chan dreamed of writing poems. What do you dream of doing?

• For this activity, you will write a journal entry about what you dream of doing. Also tell how you could make your dream happen.

Prewriting

First, think of two things you dream of doing. For each one, tell how you could make your dream come true.

My Dream	How It Could Come True

Writing

Now, use another sheet of paper to write your journal entry.

35

Thinking About

Summarizing

Read the selection below. As you read, think about the ideas presented. Try to summarize the selection as you read.

Water is all around us. Some water is in rivers, streams, and lakes. This water can be treated so that it is good for people to drink. Some water drains through the soil and collects in underground pools. People can drill wells deep in the earth to pump out this water to drink. When animals want a drink of water, they go to the shores of rivers, streams, and lakes. Most people turn on the water at a sink or drinking fountain to drink.

Water reaches the earth as rain or snow. If there is enough rain or snow, then everyone has enough water to drink.

When you read the selection, you probably thought about many different things. Check the boxes next to what you thought of while you read.

I thought about how important water is.

☐ Water is in lakes and rivers.

☐ Animals need water, too.

☐ The water we drink comes from rain and snow.

What else did you think of as you read?

_____

_____

_____

_____

Read and Think

- Read the selections that follow.
- Stop at each box and answer the question.
- Remember to summarize as you read.

TALKING WITH HORSES

By Joy Parise

Let's Read

This selection tells how horses communicate. Read the selection to learn how horses let you know what they are thinking and feeling.

Horses talk to one another. They whinny, nicker, snort, blow, and neigh. Horses also talk without making a sound. They communicate with one another and with us through gestures and expressions. That's what we call body language.

Zenobia looks as if she's trying to speak. Actually, her medicine has a strange taste.

People use body language, too. We can say yes or no by nodding our heads or shaking them. We shrug our shoulders. We wave hello or good-bye. We wink when we have a secret. And we talk without speaking in many other ways as well.

A horse's body language can be obvious or subtle. It can be a strong kick or just a change in the expression of an eye.

1   How do horses communicate?

These horses seem to be saying, "Scratch my back and I'll scratch yours."

Expressive Ears

When a horse has its ears straight forward and doesn't move them, it is curious and alert. We call this pricking the ears. A horse typically pricks its ears when it knows its breakfast is coming, when it hears a strange noise, or when it meets another horse for the first time.

This horse has pricked its ears.

When a horse turns its ears to the side or halfway back, the horse is listening. It can listen with one or both ears. If the noise is on the right, the horse moves its right ear. If the sound is on the left, the horse moves its left ear. When a horse moves both ears back and forth, it's paying attention to the activity around it.

If a horse flattens its ears against the top of its head, it is showing anger. We say that the horse is pinning its ears. Sometimes a horse will pin its ears if breakfast comes too late. A horse may also pin its ears to say, "Stay away!"

This horse is listening to the left.

2 What is this section about?

Meaningful Looks

A horse that is relaxed and happy will have a "soft" eye, which looks round and kind. A horse that is unhappy will glare with a "hard" eye, which looks oval, angry, and mean.

A horse has a hard eye when something is bothering it. Maybe the horse has a pain in the back or in a leg. Or maybe the horse didn't sleep well. If a horse has both a hard eye and pinned ears, watch out!

When white shows around a horse's eyes, it is frightened or anxious. Usually when a horse is white-eyed, a handler talks to it in a low, kind voice. Sometimes this tone of voice can make a horse feel more comfortable, and its eyes begin to soften.

3 What did you learn about a horse's eyes?

This horse has a soft eye.

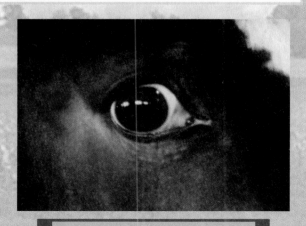

This horse has a white eye.

41

Kicking

Do horses kick when they are angry? Not always. A horse sometimes kicks to get flies off its stomach or legs. Sometimes it kicks its stall to tell someone to hurry up with breakfast. Horses in a field may kick and buck while they are playing. Horses also kick at their bellies if they have a stomachache.

4   How do horses use their legs to show you how they feel?

Sometimes horses kick just for fun.

Tails Tell Tales

A horse also talks with its tail. The happy, relaxed horse usually holds its tail still. If there are flies around, it will swish its tail in a relaxed and rhythmic manner to chase the flies away.

A horse that is playing in a field may arch its tail high, almost over its back. This shows that the horse is feeling good. Some parade horses also lift their tails as they show off for the crowd.

If a horse swishes its tail when there are no flies, the horse is bored or impatient. A horse will snap and twist its tail when it's angry. This sign is called wringing the tail. Sometimes a horse clamps down its tail to say that its back hurts or that someone has touched a sore spot.

 5 How does a horse communicate with its tail?

This horse seems proud of its beautiful mane and tail.

Now that you know a little bit about how horses communicate, you can learn more for yourself—even if you have no horses nearby. Body language is common among many kinds of animals, including dogs, cats, and other pets. Watch the animals around you. What do you think they are trying to say?

6   How was this article organized?

"Any treats?"

Time to Write!

Imagine that your class is doing a science project on how people and animals communicate without talking. You have been assigned to do your report about how people communicate.
- For this activity, you will write a report about the different ways that people communicate without talking.

Prewriting

First, think of how to organize your report. Use the questions below to help.

What feelings can I show with my face?

Feelings	How my face looks

What feelings can I show with my arms and hands?

Feelings	How my arms and hands look

What are other ways I communicate ideas and feelings without talking?

_____

_____

_____

Writing

Now, use another sheet of paper to write your report about how people communicate.

45

Animals in Danger

By Janine Amos

Let's Read

This selection is about animals that are in danger of dying out forever. Read the selection to find out why the animals are in danger and what can be done to save them.

What Does Endangered Mean?

The dodo was a short, fat bird the size of a large turkey. It had a curly tail and tiny wings. You will never see a live dodo. The very last one died over three hundred years ago. Dodos are extinct.

Today, many animals are in trouble. They are in danger of dying out forever, just like the dodo. We call them endangered animals.

The dodo could not fly. People and animals killed dodos for food until they became extinct.

Fumes from cars and factories have poisoned the lake habitats of spotted salamanders.

Why Are Animals in Danger?

Each separate type of animal is called a species. Hundreds of new species are discovered every year, but thousands of known and unknown species are in danger of extinction. Some are harmed by poisons from factories and farms. Some are hunted for their skins. Many species begin to die out when their homes, or habitats, are destroyed.

 1 What does this section say about why animals are in danger?

Plants, Animals, People

Plants, animals, and people need each other in order to survive. They all depend on one another in the cycle of life.

People need certain animals for food and work. In turn, these animals need plants and other animals. Every time a species becomes extinct, part of this chain is broken. Other living things may be threatened, including people.

2   What does this section tell about?

Bees help fruits and vegetables to grow by carrying pollen from plant to plant.

The Changing Landscape

More and more people are born every year. There is less living space for wildlife. Forests are being cleared to build cities, factories, and roads. Huge wild areas are being turned into ranches and farms. All over the world, natural habitats are being harmed or destroyed. Hundreds of species can no longer find the food and shelter they need.

Newcomers

People can change natural habitats by moving new animals into an area. These "newcomers" may kill the animals already there or eat their food. The newcomers may take over the habitat.

People themselves are a danger to animals. Tourists and vacationers can disturb wild animals and harm their habitats.

 3   How are animals in danger from newcomers?

49

A Dirty World

Factories, cities, and traffic make the world dirty because they produce waste. This dirty waste is called pollution. Pollution from factories may drain into rivers. Sometimes fish are poisoned. Birds that eat the fish are poisoned, too. Crop spraying is another kind of pollution. Farmers spray crops to kill insect pests, but harmless animals die too.

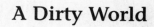

Many California condors have died from eating poisoned animal bodies.

4 What does this section say about pollution?

Dangerous Oceans

People pollute the oceans, too. They use them as giant garbage dumps. Lost fishing nets and other floating waste make dangerous traps for animals. Poisons from factories drain into the water. Sea creatures become ill and die. Oil tanker accidents spill sticky black oil into the sea, harming many animals.

Hunted!

People endanger animal species by hunting them. Some animals are hunted for their skins, which are made into clothes. Other animals are hunted for their horns and tusks. These are made into ornaments and jewelry. Some species are caught and sold as pets. They are transported to foreign countries. Many die on the way.

 5   What does this section say about why animals are in danger?

Crocodile skins are made into shoes and handbags. Three species of crocodiles are in danger of becoming extinct.

Millions of sharks are caught every year for food. Some species, like the hammerhead, may be in danger.

Hunting in the Water

Animals of the rivers and oceans are in danger from hunting, and from fishing, too. People fish for food, but sometimes so many of one species are caught that it becomes endangered. Huge nets used for fishing can trap other water animals, such as dolphins, by accident.

 6 How are animals that live in the water in danger?

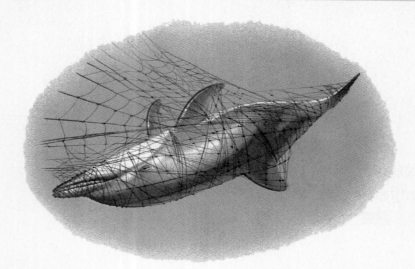

Some species of dolphin are drowned in fishing nets used to catch tuna.

What Can Be Done

 7   What is this section going to be about?

Many species of animals will only survive if we protect them and their habitats. This work is called conservation. Conservation groups in many countries are working to save endangered species. They are asking for laws to be made to protect endangered animals. They are trying to stop habitats from being polluted and destroyed.

The giant panda was once common in China. Now its habitat has to be protected.

Protected Land

Many countries have set aside land as national parks or natural preserves. In these areas, wild animals and their habitats are protected. Nobody is allowed to build there and hunting is against the law. Park managers make sure the animals are safe. In some large preserves they ride in helicopters to count the animals from above.

Komodo dragons are huge lizards. They are protected in a national park on Komodo Island in Indonesia.

Zoos

Some endangered species are protected in zoos. Here scientists can study the animals and learn more about them. Zoo workers help some animals to breed. This is called captive breeding. Sometimes it is the only way to keep a species alive. One day it may be safe to move these animals to homes in the wild.

A Last Chance

Time is running out fast for many species. Not all animals breed well in zoos. Some species must be left in the wild in protected areas. Others, like the kakapo, have to be moved away from people. The kakapo is a shy parrot that lives on the ground. Scientists have moved some of the last kakapos to lonely islands near New Zealand. Here they are safe from rats, cats, and people.

 8   What does this section tell about?

There are only about 50 kakapos left. Scientists hope they will breed on their safe island homes.

Success Stories

Endangered animals can be saved. Protection in preserves has saved the American bison from extinction. Laws to stop hunting have helped some species of seals and some tigers. The Nene goose of Hawaii was saved from extinction by captive breeding. Many have been taken home to Hawaii and live in protected areas.

The Juan Fernandez fur seal was hunted for its fur. Now it is a protected species.

Time to Write!

You just read a selection about animals in danger.

- For this activity, you will write a summary about what you read.

Prewriting

First, review the headings in the selection. Write a brief note about each heading. Use what you wrote in the boxes to help you remember.

_____

_____

_____

_____

_____

_____

_____

Writing

Now, use another sheet of paper to write your summary of "Animals in Danger."

Trees and Plants in the Rain Forest

by Saviour Pirotta

This selection tells about the trees and plants of the rain forest. Read the selection to find out about the food and products these trees and plants provide.

Rain Forests Around the World

Rain forests are thick forests in parts of the world where there is lots of rain. Most of them are near the equator, an imaginary line that runs around the center of the earth. The biggest rain forest is in the Amazon, in South America.

This rain forest is in Brazil.

Rain forests have more types of trees and plants than exist anywhere else. Since rain forests are always hot and wet, trees and plants can grow in them all year round.

 1 What is the first part of this selection about?

Rain Forest Layers

The rain forest has different layers, like a house with different floors. Different plants and animals live in each layer.

All the plants in the rain forest are especially suited to their own layer.

The top layer of the rain forest is called the canopy. It is made of the thick branches of trees tangled together.

— Canopy

Understory

Forest floor

This diagram shows the three layers of the rain forest.

Under the canopy is the understory, where bushes and smaller trees grow. There is not much light in the understory, so trees and plants grow only where light shines through.

At the bottom is the hot, dark forest floor. Fungi, ferns, and herbs grow there. They grow in a mixture of soil and dead leaves, which fall from the trees.

The forest floor is always crawling with insects and termites. Many are camouflaged to look like their surroundings.

2   What did you learn in this section?

When the fruits of the cannonball tree fall to the ground, they make a loud, booming sound.

Needing One Another

Trees, plants, and animals in the rain forest all need one another to grow. Flowering plants grow on the branches of trees high up in the canopy, where the sunshine can reach them.

The leaves of plants form little ponds for frogs, crabs, and insects to live in. Some plants feed off the bodies of dead insects. When the insects die, they become food for the plants.

Fruit trees in the canopy provide food for animals. After the animals eat the fruit, the seeds in their droppings are left on the ground. The seeds in the fruit grow into new trees.

Birds and bees feed on nectar from flowers. Without knowing it, they repay the flowers by fertilizing them with pollen. The pollen sticks to their bodies as they feed on the nectar. When the birds and bees fly to the next flower, the pollen rubs off.

A hummingbird feeds on the nectar of a flower in Costa Rica.

Fruits of the Forest

The rain forest provides lots of food for people, as well as for animals. Many juicy fruits, like bananas, mangoes, pawpaws, and star fruit grow all year round.

3 What are you thinking about now?

Next time you visit a supermarket, look around for these rain forest fruits.

Vegetables like manioc, sweet potatoes, and breadfruit are grown by farmers for their families to eat. Tea, coffee, cocoa, and cereals are grown to be sold to other countries.

A girl in Indonesia splits open the pods of cocoa fruit, to get to the fleshy nuts inside.

The buriti palm tree is very important to the people of the Amazon. It can be made into oil, starch, cork, and fiber for making string. No wonder they call it the "Tree of Life!"

Brazil nut trees grow wild in the Amazon. People collect the nuts in huge baskets and sell them in the markets.

Most Brazil nuts are sold to other countries. They are popular in countries like Great Britain and the United States.

Rubber and Chewing Gum

Thousands of families in the rain forest earn their living from one kind of tree—the rubber tree. They are called rubber tappers.

Rubber tappers make deep cuts in the tree trunk, which oozes a milky sap.

Rubber tappers collect the sap in cups. Later, they mix it with water and acid, and it turns into solid rubber. Rubber tappers sell the rubber to factories in their own country and abroad.

A rubber tapper collects sap from a rubber tree in Indonesia.

Did you know that chewing gum comes from a tree in the rain forest, too? It is called the sapodilla tree. People collect its sap, called chicle, in the same way that rubber tree sap is collected. The sap is boiled until it is hard. Then it is sent to the chewing gum factory.

A chicle tapper makes deep cuts in a sapodilla tree to drain the chicle.

4 What is this part of the selection about?

Rattan

Thousands of people in Indonesia earn their living from rattan, which is a thorny, climbing plant. Rattan can grow up to 650 ft. (200 m) long.

The thicker stems are used to make furniture. Others are split into fine strands and made into baskets or rope. Most rattan furniture is sold to other countries.

The Forest in Danger

Rain forest people are very careful to take from the forest without harming it. But new arrivals are not so careful. Settlers from the city and large companies burn down vast areas of forest for farmland and mining.

Sad to say, the new farmland does not last long. The rain washes away the soil, and the land becomes a desert. Then the settlers and companies move on to burn more forest.

Logging companies cut down thousands of trees each year. They sell the wood to countries like the United States, to be made into furniture.

Without the trees, many plants, animals, and insects lose their homes and die. Many species become extinct every day.

It takes only ten years for rain forest that has been burned to turn into desert.

65

No wonder rain forest people are fighting to save their land and trees. They know that farmers can grow crops without burning down the trees. They want loggers to cut down fewer trees, not whole areas of forest.

People in rich countries can help save the rain forests, too, by not buying things made of precious woods, like mahogany.

5   What is the main idea of this selection?

A logging company has cut down trees to be made into furniture.

Time to Write!

You just read a description of the rain forest. Think about a place where you enjoy spending time. It can be inside or outside.

• In this activity, you will write a descriptive paragraph about a place.

Prewriting

First, use the space below to help plan what you will write. Name the place in the center box. Write words or phrases that describe it in the other boxes.

Place:

Writing

Now, use another sheet of paper to describe the place.

67

Thinking Along on Tests

You have been thinking along as you read. Now practice thinking along to help you answer test questions.

Read and Think

- Read each selection.
- Stop at each box and answer the question.
- Answer the questions at the end of each selection.

How can we help?

Everyone on the block was busy. People were banging hammers everywhere as they built booths for the neighborhood street fair the next day. The fair was going to raise money for research that would help sick people.

The police had closed off one block of Sixth Street for the fair. Carlos and Danny kept walking up and down the block watching. Carlos felt very guilty. "We should have planned something," he told Danny.

They stopped to watch Jesse, Carlos's brother, and his friend Tom working on their booth. The older boys had spent weeks building a ring-toss game and making beautiful signs. They had a board with pegs that stood out on it. It was painted with bright colors and numbers for scores beside the pegs. People would pay a quarter to try to throw three rubber rings around the pegs. The names of the people with the highest scores would be written on a big chalkboard.

 1   What are you thinking about now?

The ring-toss booth looked so good that no one wanted to set up next to it. Therefore, the space next to Jesse and Tom was still empty.

"This really looks great!" Danny said. "We could never build anything like that. They are sure to win the prize for the best-looking booth."

Carlos wanted to leave. "We should have done something," he mumbled.

"We could go and collect cans to recycle," Danny said. "Then we can add the money we get for the cans to what people make at the fair."

They set off with a big plastic bag. Soon it was full, and they got another one. When they got home, they began rinsing out all the cans.

Carlos said to Danny, "You know that barrel in your garage? We could roll it out into that space beside Jesse's booth. Then we could set ten cans on top of it. You know, four on the bottom, then three on top of those, then two, and one on top. We could let people throw my old softball at them to see how many cans they can knock off the barrel."

"We only have one old softball," Danny said.

"Then they only get one throw," Carlos said. "It will go faster and we'll make more money. Ten cents a throw."

"It will dent up all the cans," Danny said.

"So what. They are going to be recycled anyway."

"We don't have prizes to give them," Danny said.

Carlos's dad said, "I'll make a batch of cookies. You can give them to whoever knocks off all the cans."

The softball throw game was a big success. Carlos and Danny worked hard all day to keep the cans set up.

At the end of the day, the boys were tired of bending over but had more money for the research than any other booth. Jesse and Tom did win the prize for the best-looking booth. However, the older boys were still there tearing it down long after Carlos and Danny had taken their barrel and cans home.

 2 What are you thinking about now?

Darken the circle before the correct answer.

1. No one wanted to set up a booth beside the ring-toss booth because _____.

   Ⓐ it was so noisy

   Ⓑ there was no space there

   Ⓒ it would not look as good

   Ⓓ it cost too much money to play

2. Why did Carlos and Danny begin collecting cans?

   Ⓐ They wanted to earn money for research.

   Ⓑ The street needed cleaning before the fair began.

   Ⓒ The cans were needed for Jesse and Tom's booth.

   Ⓓ Carlos's dad promised to give them cookies when they got back.

3. What did Danny think of Carlos's idea at first?

   Ⓐ He knew it would be easy to do.

   Ⓑ He feared it would anger Jesse and Tom.

   Ⓒ He said people would hate the game.

   Ⓓ He kept worrying about how it could work.

4. Why were Carlos and Danny tired at the end of the day of the fair?

   Ⓐ They had to spend time tearing down their booth after the fair.

   Ⓑ They had been picking up trash at the fair all day.

   Ⓒ They had to keep picking up the cans people knocked down.

   Ⓓ They had been rolling a barrel up and down the block.

Write your answer on the lines below.

5. How could someone win a cookie at Carlos and Danny's booth?

_____

_____

_____

How can you make your own panorama?

Have you ever seen a beautiful view that nearly took your breath away? Maybe you were looking out at hills when you stopped along a road. Maybe you were at the Grand Canyon. Or maybe you were in a tall building looking out over a city.

You may have wished that you could have a picture of what you were seeing. One thing that makes a view like that so beautiful is that it is very wide. Even while standing there, you cannot see it all at one time. You must turn your head in different directions. Such a wide view is called a panorama.

People have always wanted to capture pictures like that. Sometimes they painted the scene around a room. The painted picture is also called a panorama.

1   What are you thinking about now?

You can capture a panorama by using a movie or video camera. Move the camera very slowly from one side of the view to the other. But this does not show the entire panorama at the same time. Suppose you wanted a panorama of a favorite view to hang on your wall. Very expensive cameras with special lenses can capture panoramas. There is also a way you can use a regular camera and make a panorama for your wall.

Take a series of pictures, one at a time. Start at one side of the view, take a picture, move the camera just a little bit toward the other side, and take another picture. The idea is to move the camera so that each shot just touches or slightly overlaps the side of the next shot.

When you do this, it is a good idea to set your camera on something to keep it steady and level. You can use a special camera stand called a tripod because it has three legs. If you don't have a tripod, you may be able to use a post, a railing, or a table.

2   What are you thinking about now?

When you get the prints of your pictures back, you will see that you have the same parts of the view in more than one picture. There are the same buildings or trees two times or more. Cut away the parts of the view that are shown more than once. Then you can piece the pictures together in a line so that everything shows just once.

Next you can paste the pictures together in a line on a piece of poster board. It is a good idea to use a colored board that acts as a border. Cut it to fit into a long picture frame you already have.

You can trim the top and bottom edges of the pictures to make them straight across. Or, leave them uneven to show how you have put the pictures together. People will be able to see that you have created the panorama, like a piece of art. Yet it will be a real picture of the view you love.

3   What are you thinking about now?

Making your own panorama is fairly easy. Follow these steps:

1. Take your camera to the view that you like.

2. Place your camera on something to hold it steady.

3. Take several pictures. Start at one side of the view and move toward the other side. After each picture, move the camera slightly to touch or overlap the picture before.

4. Have the pictures developed and printed.

5. Line up the pictures, and cut away repeated parts to show everything in the view just once.

6. Paste the pictures on a colored poster board that fits into a frame you have.

 4 What are you thinking about now?

Darken the circle for the correct answer.

6. A panorama is a picture that _____.

   Ⓐ is very tall and narrow

   Ⓑ is very long or wide

   Ⓒ stands on three legs

   Ⓓ repeats things over and over

8. The numbered sentences at the end of this article are _____.

   Ⓐ a list of things you could photograph

   Ⓑ reasons that people like panoramas

   Ⓒ mistakes you should try not to make

   Ⓓ steps for making your own panorama

7. Which one of the following can be used to make your panorama with photos?

   Ⓐ a pair of scissors

   Ⓑ a set of water colors

   Ⓒ an album of your family

   Ⓓ a television set

9. The first thing you need to do in making a panorama is to _____.

   Ⓐ cut away unneeded parts of the picture

   Ⓑ have your pictures developed

   Ⓒ find poster board for a long frame

   Ⓓ decide what you want in your picture

Write your answer on the lines below.

10. If you make a panorama, what do you need to do when you paste the pictures to the poster board?

_____

_____

_____

What kind of sea monster is this?

Along a dock on an island in the Florida Keys, a group of campers from New England is gathered. They are *oohing* and *aahing* and pointing down into the shallow water. There, just under the dock in water only a few feet deep is a huge sea creature! Its body ends in a small head with a square snout. It does not see or hear well, so it does not swim away.

"Look! Look!" a child squeals. "It's some kind of monster!"

1 What are you thinking about now?

"Careful!" the boy's mother says. "It's as big as a cow!"

A woman from Florida smiles and says that the "creature" is often called a "sea cow."

"It is a manatee, one of the gentlest animals on earth. This one is a big adult," she explains. "Adult manatees range from 8 to 15 feet long and weigh around 1,500 pounds. But they are very gentle animals," she repeats. "They never attack anything."

The manatee stirs as it lifts its snout to the surface. The child jumps away. "The manatee has to breathe air every three to five minutes," the woman says.

"Why is it up here near the dock?" the child asks. "Is it sick?"

"No," the woman answers. "But it was injured once." She points to a big scar on the manatee's back. She explains, "Manatees like to live in shallow water. They often swim up into slow-moving Florida rivers and canals."

 2 What are you thinking about now?

The woman continues, "Manatees eat only water plants. They help keep the waterways free of plant growth that can get tangled up in the propellers of boat motors. Those boats are very dangerous for the manatee. Many of the animals are injured or killed by the propellers. Also, manatees can die when they get tangled in trash that humans throw into the water."

"A manatee spends much time feeding, and can eat 100 pounds of plants a day!" she tells the crowd.

"Is that all they do?" the boy asks.

The woman responds, "Manatees also explore the area, swimming around at less than five miles per hour. They are usually alone, but sometimes they swim in groups. They body surf and seem to play follow the leader. They communicate with each other by touching muzzles."

She points out the manatee's tail, which is shaped like a paddle. "The manatee uses its tail to steer in the shallow water. The animal can not move its head and has to turn its huge body around to see in a different direction. It has front flippers that help it turn and also bring food to its mouth."

 3   What are you thinking about now?

"The Florida manatee is one of three types of manatees in the world. In some places manatees are hunted for meat, hide, and oils. We believe there are fewer than 2,500 left," the woman explains. "They are an endangered species and could become extinct. Therefore, it is against the law to hunt them here."

"Manatees have only one baby every two to five years. The baby is called a calf and stays with its mother for about two years. Because of this, manatees are not likely to increase in number and the remaining ones need to be protected," the woman concludes.

 4 What are you thinking about now?

Darken the circle for the correct answer.

11. People call manatees "sea cows" because the animal _____.

Ⓐ stays in shallow water

Ⓑ gives people milk

Ⓒ has a large body

Ⓓ eats grass in fields

13. Boaters should watch out for manatees because these animals _____.

Ⓐ might attack the boat

Ⓑ can be injured by the boat's motor

Ⓒ always swim in big groups

Ⓓ can be used for food and oil

12. How does the manatee help boaters?

Ⓐ It eats the weeds that can get caught in their motors.

Ⓑ It stays away from docks and shallow water.

Ⓒ It frightens people who think it is a huge monster.

Ⓓ It digs canals for the boats to use.

14. The manatee must come up to the surface of the water to _____.

Ⓐ watch out for boats

Ⓑ let people know it is around

Ⓒ breathe the air it needs

Ⓓ climb up onto land

Write your answer on the lines below.

15. Describe briefly what a manatee looks like.

_____

_____

_____

_____

_____

Author's Purpose

Read the selection below. As you read, think about why the author wrote it.

Are you thinking about getting a cat for a pet? You must think about what you want. Do you want to get a little kitten or a cat that is already grown? A kitten will need someone to play with it. Do you want a cat with long hair or short hair? A cat with long hair will need to be brushed. Will your cat stay indoors or outdoors, or both? An indoor cat will need a litter box. Do you want a cat that is a certain color? Some colors are harder to find than others.

Cats have different personalities. Some like to cuddle and be petted. Others like to be left alone. What kind of cat would you like?

Why do you think the author wrote this selection? Check the boxes next to what the author was trying to tell you.

I thought the author was trying to tell me how cats act.

☐ How to pick out a cat for a pet

☐ How cats are different

☐ How to care for different cats

What else was the author trying to tell you?

_____

_____

_____

_____

Read and Think

- Read the selections that follow.
- Stop at each box and answer the question.
- Remember to think about why the author wrote the selection.

The Great Wheels Race

By Vivian C. M. Markert

Let's Read

This selection is about a race on wheels. A boy named Willie has a special set of wheels. Read the selection to find out about Willie's wheels and to learn who wins the "Great Wheels Race."

Every year Willie's neighborhood had a Great Wheels Race. Scooters, bikes, tricycles, skates, and skateboards sped all the way through the neighborhood. And every year Willie watched someone win.

But not this year. Willie was done watching. This year Willie was ready to race.

 1   Why do you think that Willie wants to race so much?

From his porch Willie saw Chico draw a green chalk starting line on the sidewalk. Willie saw all the neighborhood kids getting ready to watch the race. "Better hurry, Willie!" Chico yelled.

84

"I'll be right there!" Willie yelled back.

Gloria arrived on her red bicycle. She wore four red ribbons in her brown hair. They matched her bike. "These are my victory ribbons," she told Chico.

Willie called out, "Wait until you see *my* new victory gear." He put on his mom's bicycle helmet. Now it was a racing helmet.

Franklin arrived on his skateboard. "See how I painted on these lightning bolts! They're for speed," he told Chico and Gloria.

Willie put on his dad's swimming goggles. Now they were racing goggles. "Good-looking lightning, Franklin, but I've got something for speed, too," he shouted.

Elizabeth arrived on her in-line skates. She bent down to tighten them, saying, "See, everyone? The tighter my skates are, the better I can take the corners."

Willie put on his brother's white leather batting gloves. Now they were racing gloves. "Corners, here I come!" he yelled.

He threw open his porch door and zipped down the ramp. Everyone stared at his new sports wheelchair, all silver and shiny.

2   What does the author think is special about Willie's wheels?

"What kind of wheelchair is that?" Elizabeth asked. "Where's your old one?"

"This is the kind of wheelchair that's going to leave you all behind," Willie said. "This chair's *wild.*"

"You look different, too," Franklin said.

"I've been pumping iron all winter," Willie said, flexing his arms. His muscles bulged.

"O.K.!" Chico said. "Line up! Remember—you go down the alley, around the corner, through the park, past the wading pool, then up the big hill to my house. Then we'll know whose wheels are the coolest."

"One!" Chico shouted. The racers all leaned forward. "Two!" he yelled. The crowd jumped up and down. "Three!" Chico shouted. He raised a red flag. "Go!"

Willie, Elizabeth, Franklin, and Gloria took off in a cloud of dust and gravel. Neck and neck, wheel to wheel, they tore down the alley. The crowd ran behind them, cheering.

"Watch out for the corner!" someone yelled.

Willie slowed down and took the corner on both wheels. He barely missed the sweet lilac bushes as he rolled by.

Everyone else slowed down, too, except Gloria.

Crash!

Down the sidewalk the racers rolled. It was Franklin on his skateboard, Elizabeth on her skates, Willie in his wild wheelchair, and last of all, Gloria with lilacs in her hair.

 3 Why do you think that Gloria ran into the lilac bush?

"They're at the park!" someone yelled.

Willie slapped his wheels hard. The park passed by in a blur. He ducked under the willow trees. Leaves and branches whipped his helmet and goggles. Everyone else sped up and ducked under the willow trees, too. Almost everyone—except Franklin.

Crash!

Through the rest of the park they raced. It was Elizabeth on her skates, Willie in his wild wheelchair, Gloria with lilacs in her hair, and last of all, Franklin wrapped in willow branches.

"Look out for the pool!" someone shouted.

Instead of taking a shortcut through the gate and across the pool deck, Willie went the long way around the fence. The grass and mud pulled at his wheels. Everyone took the long way—except Elizabeth.

Splash!

 4 Why do you think Franklin and Elizabeth crashed?

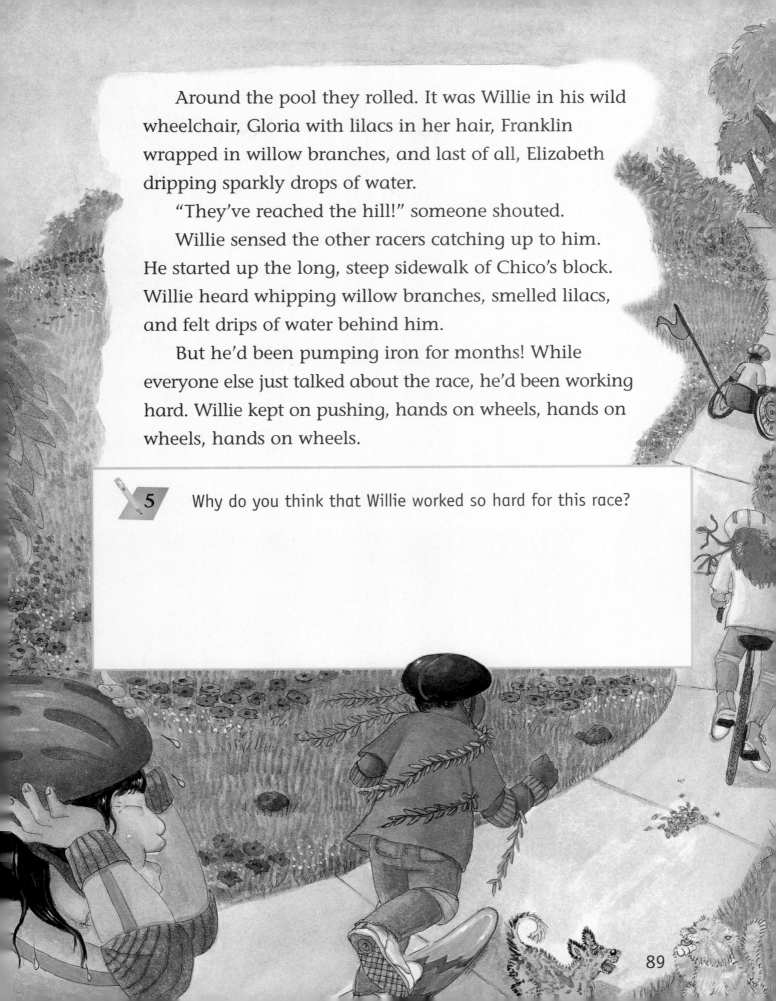

Around the pool they rolled. It was Willie in his wild wheelchair, Gloria with lilacs in her hair, Franklin wrapped in willow branches, and last of all, Elizabeth dripping sparkly drops of water.

"They've reached the hill!" someone shouted.

Willie sensed the other racers catching up to him. He started up the long, steep sidewalk of Chico's block. Willie heard whipping willow branches, smelled lilacs, and felt drips of water behind him.

But he'd been pumping iron for months! While everyone else just talked about the race, he'd been working hard. Willie kept on pushing, hands on wheels, hands on wheels, hands on wheels.

5 Why do you think that Willie worked so hard for this race?

Willie could hardly breathe! But he kept on going. Willie's hands hurt! But he kept on going. Willie's chair jolted over sidewalk cracks! But he kept on going.

Willie rolled over a thick red chalk line on the sidewalk. And he kept on going.

"Stop!" Chico yelled. "Come back, Willie! You won! You won!"

And it was Willie who won, in his wild wheelchair.

6 Why do you think the author had Willie win the race?

Imagine that you are a TV sports reporter. You are reporting on a race. It can be running, swimming, bicycling, or another kind of race.
- For this activity, you will create a TV sports report about a race.

Prewriting

First, think of the details you will include in your report.

What kind of race is it? _____

Where does the race take place? _____

What happens during the race that makes it exciting? _____

_____

_____

_____

Who wins the race? _____

How do the people in the race feel at the end? _____

_____

_____

_____

Writing

Now, use another sheet of paper to write your TV sports report.

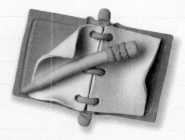

91

Small Dog Blues

By Bonnie Brightman

This selection is about a boy named Ricky who wants a dog. Unfortunately, the dog he is given is not exactly what Ricky is expecting. Read the selection to find out about Ricky's new dog.

"Lobo!" Ricky shouted. "That's it. I'll name him Lobo!"

Ricky was lying on his bed, trying to think of a name for the dog Mama was bringing home today. The name had to have a big sound—something like Bang or Pow, but in Spanish. Yes, Lobo was perfect.

> *Lobo* means "wolf."

"Enrique, your mama's back. She's got the dog!" Abuela called from the living room. "I can see them out the window!"

> *Abuela* is Spanish for "grandmother."

"Already?" Ricky cried. He jumped up and sped out of his room to the front of their apartment. Ricky stretched his arms wide and braced his feet, ready for his big furry dog to come bounding through the door.

What kind of dog would it be? Ricky wondered. Mama had finally agreed they needed a dog for protection. So it would have to be very big, wouldn't it? Something fierce, like a Doberman. Uncle Luis had one of those, and it once shredded the whole front seat of his Camaro while he was talking on a pay phone to his girlfriend, Conchi. Conchi had told Uncle Luis that if he ever wanted to see her again, he'd have to get rid of that dog first. No, it wouldn't be a Doberman. Maybe a German shepherd though.

Abuela opened the door.

 1   Why do you think that Ricky expects to get a big dog?

"At last, my very own . . . Lobo?" Ricky gulped. A tiny, worried-looking dog sat obediently at Mama's feet. It was shivering from the cold.

"What's this?" Ricky asked in surprise. "Where's the dog?" He looked at Mama and then at Abuela. "You promised that we'd get a dog, Mama. You said a *dog*, not a . . . a . . ." Ricky didn't know what to call the thing until it yipped at him. "Not a chicken that barks!" he finished in disgust.

"This isn't a chicken," Mama said calmly. "It's a Chihuahua. The man at the pound said Chihuahuas were the royal breed of Mexico. They're known for their bravery."

Abuela clapped her hands. "Chihuahuas come from Mexico, just like me!" She bent down and patted the dog, smiling broadly.

2   How do you think that Ricky feels about the dog?

Ricky picked up the little dog and frowned at it. The Chihuahua wagged its tail happily.

"Tell you what," Mama said. "We'll try it out until Monday. Then, if you want, I'll take it back and find a different dog. Deal?"

"Deal," said Ricky. Monday was only three days off. In the meantime, he wasn't going to name this little squirt Lobo. He'd save that name for his real dog.

Mama handed Ricky the leash. "It needs a walk."

"How embarrassing!" muttered Ricky as he skulked down the street. With a little luck, nobody would see him.

But luck was not with Ricky. He could see Stevie Reynoso in the distance. Stevie was an O.K. kid, but he was known for two things: the lies he told and his dog, el Toro. Last week, Stevie had told the whole class that he'd just been chosen World Karate King. Ricky called him Stevie Reynoso, el Mentiroso—except when el Toro was around.

> *El toro* means "the bull."

> *El mentiroso* means "the liar."

3   What are you thinking about now?

El Toro was pulling Stevie down the street at a gallop. Ricky watched with envy. El Toro was undoubtedly the biggest dog alive. He was so big that Stevie couldn't control him. As a result, Stevie was yelling at him. Ricky figured that was what made el Toro so mean. He would growl if you just looked at him.

El Toro had seen Ricky and was headed straight for him. Ricky scooped up the Chihuahua and stuck it down inside his jacket.

"What's up?" asked Stevie.

"Not much." Ricky shrugged. "What's up with you?"

"Just taking el Toro for his walk. Want to come?" asked Stevie.

"Uh, no thanks," said Ricky. The Chihuahua wiggled its way up into Ricky's armpit, making Ricky laugh.

"What's so funny?" asked Stevie. "El Toro doesn't like it when people laugh." El Toro gave a low growl. Stevie struggled to hold him back.

"Nothing," said Ricky. The Chihuahua yipped faintly. "Quiet, you," Ricky hissed into the top of his jacket.

4 Why do you think Ricky holds his new dog in his jacket?

"Huh?" said Stevie, looked suspiciously at Ricky.

Suddenly el Toro spotted a large black cat sitting on a Dumpster halfway down the street.

"Whoa!" Stevie shrieked.

El Toro charged toward the cat, which was now climbing a nearby chain-link fence. El Toro lunged up the fence. He might have caught the cat if not for Stevie's dead weight at the other end of his leash.

"Whew," Ricky said as he pulled the Chihuahua from under his armpit and set it on the ground. "That was close. We wouldn't want el Toro making a snack of you, would we?" Of course, Ricky's real reason for hiding the Chihuahua was that he didn't want Stevie to see what a runt it was.

The living room was cold when Ricky got up early Sunday morning to watch TV. He laid his sleeping bag on the floor and crawled in. The little Chihuahua crawled in, too. It scrambled to the bottom of the bag and curled itself around Ricky's feet.

"You're a pretty good heater," Ricky said into his sleeping bag. The dog snored happily. "It's nothing personal, you know," Ricky went on, feeling guilty about his plan to give the dog back. "You're going to be a great dog for the right person." The dog snored some more. Ricky smiled and turned back to his program.

 5 Why do you think the author has the dog "curl up" with Ricky?

The next afternoon, Ricky put on his jacket to take the dog for a walk. The thermometer outside the living room window read zero. Ricky looked worriedly at the dog sitting patiently by the door.

"Ricky, look what I made for your friend," said Abuela. "It's a sweater! Isn't it cute?" she asked, holding it up for Ricky to see. It was bright red with navy blue tassels hanging from the neck.

Ricky looked from the sweater to the Chihuahua. Sweaters were for sissy dogs only. Even Ricky would not wear a sweater if he could get away with it. On the other hand, it was cold outside, and he could not always carry the dog under his armpit.

"I know it's embarrassing, fella," he said to the Chihuahua as he pulled the sweater over its head and pushed it out the door. "But you'll freeze solid if you don't wear something."

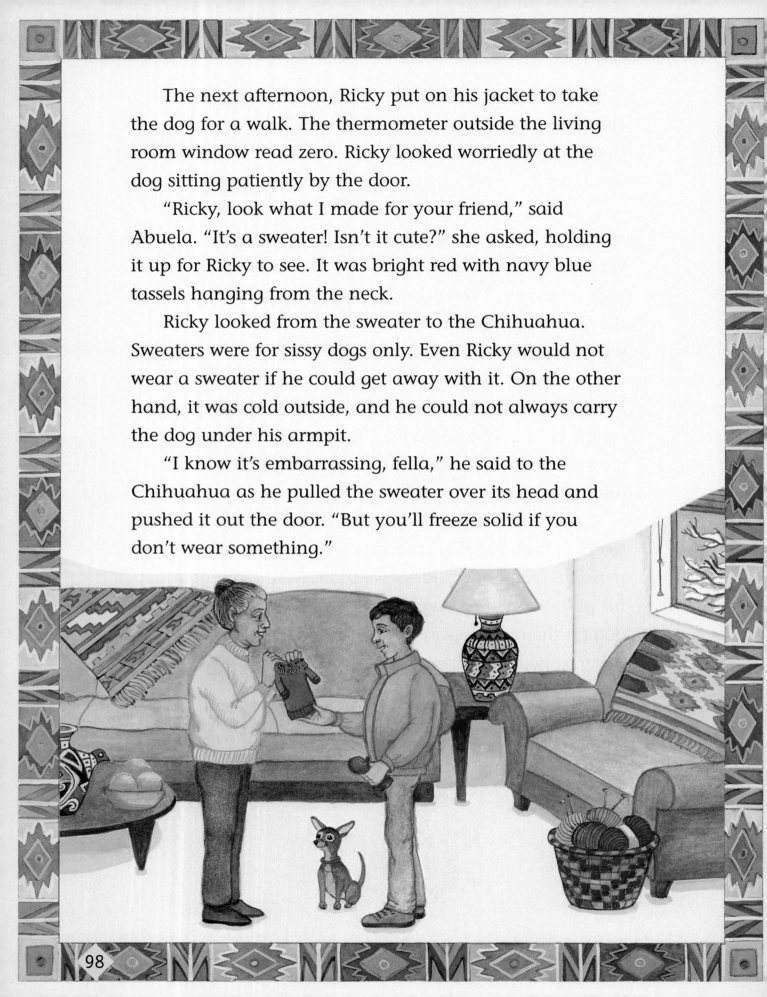

It was a quiet, cold afternoon. Anybody with a warm place to go was inside. This suited Ricky fine. If no one was out, no one would ask him why he was walking a chicken in a sweater. Yes, this would work out O.K. Tomorrow he'd be getting a big dog—something that he could name Lobo—and this little temporary dog would find a good home. Maybe a home with some nice abuela.

6 What are you thinking about now?

"So that's what you had in your jacket yesterday!" boomed a voice. Ricky had not heard Stevie and el Toro coming up behind him.

"Yeah, so?" asked Ricky, startled. Despite the cold, Ricky began to sweat as el Toro circled the Chihuahua, curling back his lips and showing his teeth. But before Ricky could scoop up the Chihuahua, it leaned toward the big dog and started to yip fiercely. El Toro sat down and wagged his tail.

"That's a cool little dog you've got there, Ricky," Stevie said.

"Well," Ricky answered proudly, "he's a Chihuahua. Chihuahuas were the royal dogs of Mexico, you know. They're known for their bravery."

"It must be nice to have a dog that doesn't pull you over all the time," Stevie said, shooting a look at el Toro.

"They're good heaters, too," Ricky answered. He picked the Chihuahua up and tucked it inside his jacket. The little dog popped its head out under Ricky's chin and looked el Toro straight in the eye.

"Actually," Ricky admitted, "I was pretty surprised when I first got it. I thought it'd be a lot . . . well . . . different."

The two boys continued walking their dogs together.

"What's its name?" asked Stevie.

"Lobo," said Ricky.

7 How do you think Ricky feels about his dog now?

Time to Write!

Imagine that a newspaper is having an essay contest. The writer of the best essay wins the perfect pet.

• For this activity, you will write an essay describing the pet you hope to win and why it would be perfect for you.

Prewriting

Use the idea web below to help plan what you are going to include in your essay. Write the kind of pet you choose in the circle.

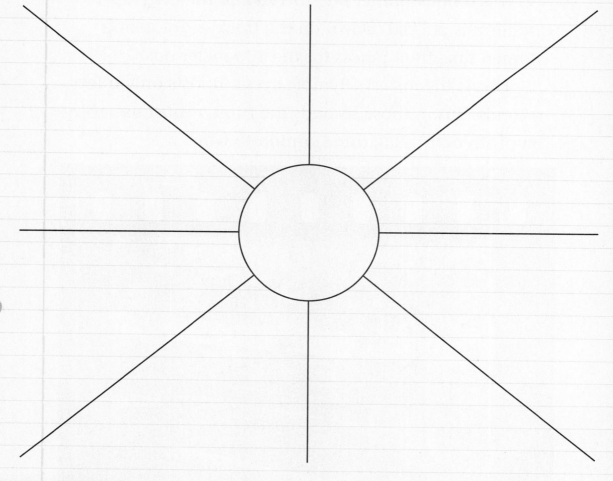

Writing

Now, use another sheet of paper to write your essay to enter the perfect pet contest.

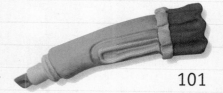

Wilma Rudolph

By Jim O'Connor

This selection tells the life story of a special woman named Wilma Rudolph. Read the selection to find out what Wilma Rudolph did that made her so special.

It is a hot summer day in 1960. Rome's Olympic Stadium is packed. Down on the track, eight young women take their places for the 100-meter dash.

This is the fastest Olympic event. It lasts only a few seconds. But in those seconds the runner must use every bit of strength, skill, and stamina to win.

When the race is over, a tall, thin black woman from the United States has won. She is awarded the first of the three gold medals she will take home. Her name is Wilma Rudolph. By the time the Olympics end, she is called the "Fastest Woman in the World."

Wilma made it all look easy. Few people could have guessed the incredible obstacles this star athlete had faced. Poverty. Prejudice. And a deadly disease that left her disabled for most of her childhood.

 1 Why do you think the author chose to write about Wilma Rudolph?

Wilma was born in Tennessee in 1940. She grew up in a small town called Clarksville. Her parents already had 16 other children. They were very poor.

Wilma was a tiny, sickly baby, but she hung on. Then at four Wilma came down with a terrible illness called polio.

From the 1930s through the early 1950s, polio killed thousands of children and left many more in wheelchairs. The "lucky" ones could only walk with their legs in iron braces.

Polio damaged Wilma's left leg. Doctors said she would walk with a brace for the rest of her life. But Wilma's mother refused to believe them. She took Wilma to a hospital where specialists worked to make Wilma's leg stronger.

 2 What are you thinking about now?

In the 1950s, blacks could not eat in the same restaurants or go to the same schools or hospitals as whites. Wilma and her mother had to travel 50 miles each way for Wilma's treatments. They did it for years.

The treatments were painful. Wilma's leg was stretched and rubbed. And every night Wilma's mother or one of her brothers or sisters stretched and rubbed the leg some more.

When Wilma started first grade, she still wore the brace. She hated it. The brace was heavy and ugly. Its leather straps hurt.

Wilma felt bad. While her friends ran and jumped and played games, she could only sit and watch. Some kids made fun of her.

3 Why do you think the author tells about Wilma Rudolph's childhood disability?

Wilma's family would cheer her up and encourage her. Slowly her leg started to get stronger. She began taking off the brace when she was at home. By the time she was ten, Wilma only had to wear it to school. And on one unforgettable day two years later, she took off the brace and never used it again.

Now at last Wilma could get off the sidelines and into the action. She decided to play basketball. Wilma was a natural on the court. In high school she scored 32 points in her first varsity game!

And the team made it to the state conference championships with Wilma as its star. They didn't win, but that tournament was very important for Wilma.

 4 What are you thinking about now?

A track coach for Tennessee State University, Ed Temple, saw Wilma play. Right away he knew her long legs and skinny build were perfect for a sprinter— someone who can run short distances very fast.

He invited Wilma to spend the summer at Tennessee State with other high school girls learning about track. In a few short weeks, she learned the secrets of sprinting: how to time her start, how to breathe properly, how to move her arms and legs correctly. She trained hard and got stronger and faster.

Her summer in Nashville paid off. Wilma ran against the nation's best young runners at the Amateur Athletic Union (AAU) championships in Philadelphia. And she won two events!

Best of all, she got to meet Jackie Robinson. Jackie was the first black man to play major-league baseball and a true superstar. Jackie told her something she never forgot: "Don't let anything or anybody keep you from running."

Then Wilma qualified for the 1956 Olympic Games in Melbourne, Australia!

At 16 she was the youngest member of the team. Wilma felt bad about beating older runners and maybe hurting their feelings. But another runner, Mae Faggs, helped Wilma develop a winning attitude. Mae made her see that it was all right to win no matter who she beat. That was what being the best meant.

 5   Why do you think the author tells about Wilma meeting Jackie Robinson?

At the '56 Olympics, Wilma saw athletes of all colors and cultures compete. And the women's 400-meter relay team, with Wilma running third, staged an upset and took the bronze medal for third place.

When Wilma returned to Clarksville with her Olympic medal, she was surprised to find that she was a hometown star! People, even white people, stopped her on the street and shook her hand. There was a ceremony in her honor.

After high school Wilma went to Tennessee State University on a full scholarship. College was tough for Wilma, but she made a "B" average and became the fastest sprinter on the Tennessee State Tigerbelles squad.

6   What are you thinking about now?

By the 1960 Olympics, Wilma was the best woman sprinter in America. She easily qualified for the 100- and 200- meter dashes. And she and three other Tigerbelles qualified for the 400-meter relay.

When the U.S. team got to Rome, the temperature was almost 100°F. But the heat didn't bother the Tigerbelles—the weather was the same back home.

Just before the games began, Wilma twisted her ankle. But that didn't stop her. She breezed into the 100-meter finals. She won her first gold medal by running the 100 meters in a blazing 11.0 seconds. In the 200 meters, she took another gold.

Wilma's final event was the 400-meter relay. The relay is a tricky race. Each of the first three runners must sprint 100 meters before handing a short stick, called a baton, to the next runner. The last runner, or "anchor," finishes the race. If the baton is dropped, the entire team is disqualified.

 7 What do you think will happen next?

Wilma was the anchor. She nearly lost the baton when it was passed to her. Then she overtook the Russian and German runners to win! "The feeling of accomplishment welled up inside of me," Wilma later recalled. "Three Olympic gold medals. I knew that was something no one could ever take away."

Wilma became world famous. In France they called her "La Perle Noire" (The Black Pearl). Italy named her "La Gazzèlla Nera" (The Black Gazelle).

When Wilma returned to the United States, she met President John F. Kennedy and toured the country.

 8   What are you thinking about now?

Clarksville had a homecoming parade for her. And there was a big dinner in her honor. It was the first time in the history of Clarksville that blacks and whites ate together.

Wilma graduated from Tennessee State in 1963. Over the next years she married, taught elementary school, coached track, and raised a family. She became one of the best known and most respected women ever to run track in the United States.

 9   Why do you think Wilma Rudolph became so well known and respected?

Time to Write!

Wilma's hometown had a parade and dinner for her. Imagine that you have been asked to give a speech at a dinner to honor her or someone else who overcame hardships to achieve success.

• For this activity, you will write a speech telling of someone's hardships and achievements.

Prewriting

First, complete the lists below to gather information for your speech.

Hardships   **Achievements**

_____

_____

_____

_____

_____

_____

_____

Writing

Now, use another sheet of paper to write your speech in honor of someone who overcame hardships to achieve success.

113

Thinking Along on Tests

You have been thinking along as you read. Now practice thinking along to help you answer test questions.

Read and Think

- Read each selection.
- Stop at each box and answer the question.
- Answer the questions at the end of each selection.

What made Corky's story scary?

One summer night, the neighborhood kids were gathered on the steps behind Amy's apartment building. The steps went down to a patio where Corky was standing in the dark. He was taking his turn at storytelling, looking up at his audience on the steps.

Corky loved to tell scary stories. His stories were actually mysteries because you could never be sure what was going to happen. Sometimes Shanell wished Corky wasn't so good at it. "Why does a mystery have to make you feel so creepy?" she thought to herself.

Shanell hugged herself as she listened. Corky was telling how a girl named Millie was lost in a big old castle.

"She had trouble getting used to the light of the torches," Corky said. "They kept flickering, and she couldn't see the bumpy stones on the steps that curved around the inside of the tower."

Shanell shivered. She had become Millie, lost in the old castle. Corky had a way of making her feel like that. The whole audience on the steps was stirring uneasily.

 1 What are you thinking about now?

"One of the torches behind Millie burned out," Corky said. His voice was tight and sounded nervous. "But she kept going down the dark stairs. She had to find her friend Jackson. He might be in trouble. If she found him, maybe together they could find their way out of this awful place. Another torch farther down burned out, and Millie could barely see where she was going."

It was getting darker on Amy's patio. Shanell could barely see Corky's face. Someone behind her moved and gently kicked her in the back.

Corky was talking in a loud whisper telling how Millie kept descending, one slow, careful step at a time. "She held out a hand, touching the stone wall to help her find her way. The stones were wet and slimy. Suddenly, the last torch burned out. Millie stopped, wondering if she could go on."

Corky's voice got a bit louder. "Just then, something fuzzy brushed against her face...."

"Heeeelllllp!"

Shanell's body felt as if she had just jumped into a pool of ice! The horrible shriek had come from the front of the building. Corky rushed past her and through the gate to the front sidewalk. Everyone followed him, with Shanell last.

 2   What are you thinking about now?

Out on the front sidewalk, a woman was waving her arms and trying to scream again. Amy's big, goofy dog, Candel, was scampering around the woman, jumping up and trying to lick her face. Candel had gotten out of the apartment and had run down the front steps looking for Amy. He found the woman instead.

Amy took Candel back inside while the other children talked to the woman. They helped her calm down. Then she went on her way, looking back to be sure the dog wasn't following.

"Time to go back and help Millie find her friend," someone said.

"No, thanks," Shanell said, heading home. "I've had enough chills for one night."

 3   What are you thinking about now?

Darken the circle before the correct answer.

1. Candel is the name of _____.

   Ⓐ the girl in Corky's story

   Ⓑ Amy's dog

   Ⓒ the woman on the front sidewalk

   Ⓓ Corky's friend

2. In this story, the word <u>descended</u> means _____.

   Ⓐ went downward

   Ⓑ whispered softly

   Ⓒ had ancestors

   Ⓓ passed by

3. Shanell thinks that Corky's story is _____.

   Ⓐ boring

   Ⓑ frightening

   Ⓒ silly

   Ⓓ pleasant

4. Why does the woman scream?

   Ⓐ Corky's story frightens her.

   Ⓑ She sees all of the children.

   Ⓒ She is scared of the dog.

   Ⓓ The torches all go out.

Write your answer on the lines below.

5. How does Shanell feel as she listens to Corky's story?

_____

_____

_____

_____

Why does everyone love Amelia?

America's love affair with Amelia Earhart never seems to end. It began when she was the first woman to cross the Atlantic Ocean in an airplane. That was in 1928. It was a year after Charles Lindbergh had been the first person to fly across that ocean alone.

Amelia was 30 years old when she crossed the Atlantic, but she was not the pilot. Wilmer Stultz flew the plane from Canada to Wales, a part of Great Britain. Amelia was just a passenger in the plane, which was named *Friendship*.

When the plane landed, Amelia Earhart was the one who got the attention of the world. Thousands of people were waiting to welcome her. Amelia did not feel that she should get all the attention. However, that same year she flew a plane across the U.S.—in both directions! She was the first woman to do that alone. She had become a famous pilot.

 1   What are you thinking about now?

In 1930, Amelia Earhart set three world speed records for women pilots. In 1932, she flew across the Atlantic alone. She had always wanted to earn the attention she had received as a passenger. Again, thousands of people were waiting for her plane to arrive. This time she landed in Ireland. When she got back to New York City, the city held a big parade for her.

In 1935, Amelia flew solo from Hawaii to California. It was a longer trip than the one across the Atlantic. Other pilots had tried but had failed. Amelia succeeded.

Amelia got many awards. She was a guest of President Franklin Roosevelt and his wife Eleanor at the White House many times. By 1937, she was ready to try to become the first woman to fly around the world.

2   What are you thinking about now?

Amelia had been teaching at Purdue University in Indiana, so Purdue paid to have a plane built for Amelia. It was a beautiful silver plane, a twin-engine Electra.

Much preparation was needed to get ready for the flight around the world. The trip could not be non-stop, of course. Amelia would fly numerous "legs," stopping in several places for rest, repairs, and gasoline. Fred Noonan would be in the plane too, as her navigator.

In May 1937, they took off from California. Amelia flew to Miami and then to South America. From there she flew to Africa, Arabia, and Pakistan. Then she flew the Electra to Australia and New Guinea. She had completed about two-thirds of the trip—23,000 miles in six weeks. However, the next leg of the trip was the most difficult because Amelia had to find a small island in the huge Pacific Ocean.

Heading across the Pacific Ocean toward that tiny island, Amelia Earhart's Electra disappeared. The world was shocked and very sad. The plane with Amelia and Fred Noonan was never found.

 3 What are you thinking about now?

The first biography of Amelia Earhart was published in 1939. Since then, many books have been written about her. Today, we still do not know what happened to Amelia Earhart. Her disappearance remains a great mystery.

America is still in love with Amelia Earhart. At the end of the 1990s, people were still writing long, loving articles about her and her mysterious end.

 4   What are you thinking about now?

Darken the circle before the correct answer.

6. **The first time that Amelia Earhart crossed the Atlantic Ocean in a plane, she _____.**
   - Ⓐ piloted the plane alone
   - Ⓑ disappeared in the plane
   - Ⓒ was just a passenger
   - Ⓓ landed in Ireland

8. **The word <u>solo</u> in this selection means _____.**
   - Ⓐ as the navigator
   - Ⓑ while singing a song
   - Ⓒ without seeing
   - Ⓓ by herself

7. **What is mysterious about Amelia?**
   - Ⓐ We don't know what happened to her.
   - Ⓑ She never flew a plane by herself.
   - Ⓒ She always drew big crowds.
   - Ⓓ She disappeared in Indiana.

9. **Why did Amelia feel she earned the attention she got in 1932?**
   - Ⓐ She flew across the Atlantic alone that year.
   - Ⓑ New York City had a big parade for her.
   - Ⓒ Lots of people welcomed her to Ireland.
   - Ⓓ She was the first woman to cross the Atlantic as a passenger.

Write your answer on the lines below.

10. **Choose what you think is Amelia's greatest accomplishment. Explain why you think it is the most important thing she did.**

_____

_____

_____

_____

Would you like to keep a journal?

Do you keep a journal? You "keep a journal" by regularly writing down your thoughts. It is a wonderful way to practice writing, and thinking as well. It can also be a good way to get to know yourself.

Writers who keep journals go to them to find ideas they had earlier and can use in new writing. It is a better way to keep ideas than just remembering them.

How is a journal different from a diary?

A diary is a record of what happens every day. Even when nothing much happens, you usually make a note about that in a diary. The idea is to keep a record of the daily events of your life.

A journal is sometimes like a diary because you can describe something that happened. But, in a journal you can write about anything else you want, as well. It doesn't have to be something that happened to you. It can be a poem or a story. It can be notes about something that interests you or how you feel about something that happened.

 1   What are you thinking about now?

When should you write in a journal?

What you write is one thing that makes a journal different from a diary. Another is that you write in a journal often and regularly, but not every single day. You might write twice a day or once this week and four times next week. You write when you have a good idea or think of something you want to remember.

What does a journal look like?

A journal is like a book, but it doesn't have to be a book. It can be a notebook or a pad. It can be sheets of paper you write on and keep together. The sheets can be stapled or just kept in order.

 2   What are you thinking about now?

A journal can have a special cover, but that isn't necessary. Some people enjoy using a book with plain or lined pages as a journal. The cover or the first page may say "My Journal" and then your name.

It is not important to have dates already printed on the pages, like in a diary. However, you should start by writing the date each time you add your thoughts.

What do you write in a journal?

You can write anything you want in a journal. You can write about something or somebody you saw. You can describe anything. You can tell how you feel about someone or something that happened.

You can make a note about something you want to remember. It can be about something you heard or read. It is a good idea to tell why you think it is important.

You can even have another person write in your journal. This is called a dialogue journal. You write something for someone in particular to read. Then, that person reads it and writes back to you—in the journal. In this way the journal is like a box of letters or notes between two people.

Who is supposed to read your journal?

The answer is simple: anyone you want. You can write just to yourself. Or you can write hoping—even knowing—that other people will read your journal. Many journals have been published as books. Some of them have very famous and wonderful writing in them. Someday, yours may be one of those!

 3 What are you thinking about now?

Darken the circle before the correct answer.

11. **Suppose you have decided to keep a journal and want to know what this article tells you about what kind of paper to use. Which heading should you look under?**

    (A) *How is a journal different from a diary?*

    (B) *When should you write in a journal?*

    (C) *What does a journal look like?*

    (D) *What do you write in a journal?*

12. **You can tell that whoever wrote this thinks that keeping a journal is a _____.**

    (A) waste of time

    (B) bad idea

    (C) lot of trouble

    (D) good idea

13. **What is one difference between a journal and a diary?**

    (A) There are different kinds of writing in a journal.

    (B) A journal has an entry for every day.

    (C) A journal should be read by only the person who writes it.

    (D) A journal is always bound like a book.

14. **A journal is "a wonderful way to practice ... thinking" because it _____.**

    (A) is so hard to figure out

    (B) contains your ideas

    (C) is always written in a code

    (D) must be about books you have read

Write your answer on the lines below.

15. **Describe briefly what you can write in a journal and when.**

_____

_____

_____

_____

Acknowledgments

Grateful acknowledgment is made to the following authors and publishers for the use of copyrighted materials. Every effort has been made to obtain permission to use previously published material. Any errors or omissions are unintentional.

Animals in Danger by Janine Amos. Copyright © 1992 by Franklin Watts. Reprinted by permission.

"The Great Wheels Race" by Vivian C. M. Markert. Reprinted by permission of SPIDER magazine, August 1998, Vol. 5, No. 8, © 1998 by Vivian C. M. Markert.

A Picture Book of Helen Keller by David A. Adler. Text copyright © 1990 by David A. Adler. All rights reserved. Reprinted from A PICTURE BOOK OF HELEN KELLER by permission of Holiday House, Inc.

"Small Dog Blues" by Bonnie Brightman. Reprinted by permission of CRICKET magazine, March 1998, Vol. 25, No. 7, © 1998 by Rita J. Markel.

"Talking with Horses" by Joy Parise. Copyright © 1997 by Highlights for Children, Inc., Columbus, Ohio. Reprinted by permission of Highlights for Children, Inc.

The Tiny Kite of Eddie Wing by Maxine Trottier with illustrations by Al Van Mil. Text copyright © 1995 by Maxine Trottier. Illustrations copyright © 1995 by Al Van Mil. Reprinted by permission of Stoddart Publishing Co. Limited, Don Mills, Ontario.

"To the Rescue!" by Linda Rae Apolzon. From the May 1996 issue of *Ranger Rick* magazine, with the permission of the publisher, the National Wildlife Federation. Copyright © 1996 by the National Wildlife Federation.

Trees and Plants in the Rain Forest by Saviour Pirotta. Copyright © 1998 by Wayland Publishers Ltd.

"Wilma Rudolph" by Jim O'Connor. From COMEBACK! FOUR TRUE STORIES by Jim O'Connor. Text copyright © 1992 by Jim O'Connor. Reprinted by permission of Random House, Inc.

Illustration Credits

Linda Kelen, pp. 4, 36, 82; Flora Jew, cover, pp. 6–14; Sandra Spiedel, cover, pp. 16–22, 24; Al Van Mil, pp. 26–34; David McAllister, pp. 46–56; Deb Bunnell, cover, pp. 58–66; Rebecca Merrilees, p. 59; Karen Dugan, pp. 68, 70, 74, 78, 114, 117, 124; Jennifer DeCristoforo, p. 77; Winifred Barnum-Newman, cover, pp. 84–86, 88–90; Cindy Brodie, cover, pp. 92–100; Elizabeth Wolf, p. 105.

Photography Credits

Cover Sam Dudgeon; p. 5 Rick Williams; p. 37 Rick Williams; p. 38 ©Sharon Dunn Umnik; p. 39 ©Zefa Germany/ The Stock Market; pp. 40, 41 ©Sharon Dunn Umnik; p. 42 ©Doris J. Brookes/Brookes Photography; p. 43 ©Barbara Wright/Animals Animals; p. 44 ©Sharon Dunn Umnik; p. 58 ©Fabio Colombini/Animals Animals; p. 60 ©Harold Taylor ABIPP/Oxford Scientific Films; p. 61 ©Michael Fodgen/Oxford Scientific Films; p. 62 ©Gerald S. Cubitt/Bruce Coleman Ltd.; p. 63 CORBIS/Dean Conger; p. 64 CORBIS/Macduff Everton; p. 65 ©Anne LeBastille/Bruce Coleman, Inc.; p. 66 CORBIS/Wayne Lawler; Ecoscene; p. 72 ©PhotoDisc; p. 80 ©Fred Whitehead/Animals Animals; p. 83 Rick Williams; p. 102 CORBIS/Bettmann; p. 103 Archive Photos; p. 107 CORBIS/Bettmann; p. 108 ARCHIVE PHOTOS/ Express Newspapers; pp. 109, 110 CORBIS/Bettmann; p. 111 CORBIS; pp. 112, 119, 121, 122 CORBIS/Bettmann.